The Essential Science Glossary I

A Student Reference Guide

Academic Vocabulary Builders

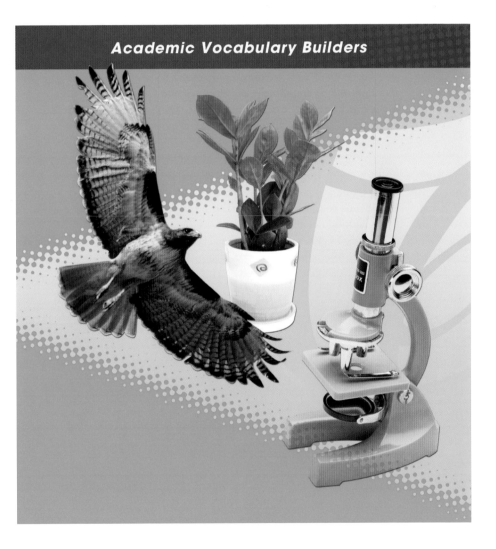

Capstone press®

Mankato, Minnesota

Academic Vocabulary Builders are published by Capstone Press,
151 Good Counsel Drive, P.O. Box 669, Mankato, Minnesota 56002.
www.capstonepress.com

Library of Congress Cataloging-in-Publication Data
The essential science glossary I : a student reference guide.
    p. cm. — (Academic vocabulary builders)
    Includes bibliographical references and index.
    Summary: "The Level I glossary covers essential content terms in the key subject area
of science for elementary level students" — Provided by publisher.
    ISBN-13: 978-1-4296-3055-9 (hardcover)
    ISBN-10: 1-4296-3055-8 (hardcover)
    1. Science — Terminology — Juvenile literature. I. Capstone Press. II. Title: Essential
science glossary 1. III. Title: Essential science glossary one. IV. Series.
Q179.E76 2009
500 — dc22   2008025677

Cover Design
Ted Williams

Design and Illustration
Sasha Blanton

1 2 3 4 5 6 13 12 11 10 09 08

Table of Contents

iii

About this book:

This book will help you learn essential words you will need to understand to do well on state tests. These essential words will also help you do well in school.

There are about 175 Science words and definitions in the book. They are listed in alphabetical order under five main topics.

Here is a sample word with its features:

Easy to read definitions

Pictures to help understanding

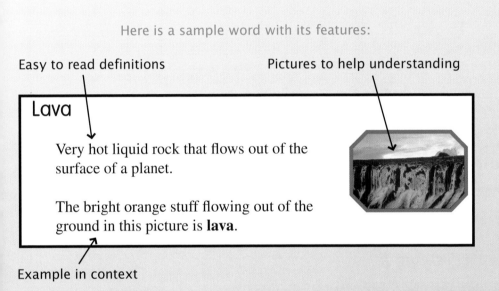

Lava

Very hot liquid rock that flows out of the surface of a planet.

The bright orange stuff flowing out of the ground in this picture is **lava**.

Example in context

Analyze

To learn about something by looking at its different parts.

Jen and Phil want to learn more about a plant. They **analyze** it by looking closely at its leaves, its stem, and its roots.

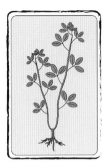

LET'S
GET
SCIENTIFIC

Conclusion

A idea that you come to based on the results of an investigation.

Bev puts a plant in the dark for a week. The plant dies. Her **conclusion** is that plants cannot grow in the dark.

THE LIVING
WORLD

THE PHYSICAL
WORLD

EARTH and SPACE

Constant

Not changing.

The sun sets every day. This is a **constant**.

TOOLS of SCIENCE

1

Cycle

Something that repeats steps in the same order.

Water moves from the Earth, into the air, and then back to the Earth again. This is a **cycle**.

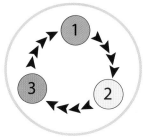

Data

Pieces of information.

Dave finds **data** about bears in a science book.

Energy

Anything that can make things happen.

It takes **energy** to make a car start up. It takes **energy** for a light to turn on.

Evaluate

To think about something carefully.

Callie and Juan **evaluate** a leaf to figure out what tree it comes from.

Evidence

Information that helps you figure out whether or not something is true.

Tara found a bug. She wanted to know what kind of bug it was. She used **evidence**, such as the bug's shape and color, to figure out what it was.

Examine

To look at something carefully.

Denise **examined** a rock. She looked at its color, its shape, and its size.

LET'S GET SCIENTIFIC

THE LIVING WORLD

THE PHYSICAL WORLD

EARTH and SPACE

TOOLS of SCIENCE

Experiment (noun)

A test.

Beth puts some plants in the dark. She is doing an **experiment** on the plants to see how well they grow in the dark.

Experiment (verb)

To test something to see what will happen.

Beth **experiments** on plants to see how they grow.

Field investigation

When you look at a living thing in its own environment.

Our class went outside to do a **field investigation** of bugs.

Hypothesis

An idea that can be tested.

I think that if I plant a seed in sand it will grow into a plant. This is my **hypothesis**.

Infer

To figure out based on what you know.

Abby and Carlos look at the size, shape, and color of a flower. They **infer** that the flower is a rose.

Interpret

To explain what you know in a way that others may also understand it.

Seth's dog's tail is wagging. He **interprets** the tail wagging to mean that the dog is happy.

LET'S GET SCIENTIFIC

THE LIVING WORLD

THE PHYSICAL WORLD

EARTH and SPACE

TOOLS of SCIENCE

LET'S
GET
SCIENTIFIC

THE LIVING
WORLD

THE PHYSICAL
WORLD

EARTH and SPACE

TOOLS of SCIENCE

Investigate

To learn about something.

Dad read a book about clouds. He wanted to **investigate** how clouds work.

Lab investigation

When you look at something in a laboratory, not its own environment.

Our class did a **lab investigation** on bugs. We found some bugs outside, put them in jars, and took them into a laboratory. We used laboratory tools to look at the bugs.

Laboratory

A place where scientists learn about things.

You can find microscopes and tools for measuring in a **laboratory**.

Measure

To figure out the exact size, weight, or height of something.

Kim and Sal **measure** a plant. They find out how much it weighs and how tall it is.

Method

The steps you take to do something.

I have a **method** for learning about rocks. First, I write down their colors. Next, I draw a picture of their shape. Finally, I find out how much they weigh and write that down, too. I do this for every rock.

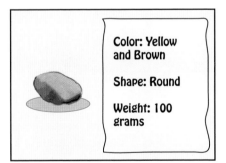

Color: Yellow and Brown

Shape: Round

Weight: 100 grams

Model

Something that looks like a real object, but is bigger or smaller or simpler.

We have a **model** of the Earth in our classroom. The real Earth is very big. Our **model** is small, but it shows what the real Earth must look like.

LET'S GET SCIENTIFIC

THE LIVING WORLD

THE PHYSICAL WORLD

EARTH and SPACE

TOOLS of SCIENCE

LET'S
GET
SCIENTIFIC

THE LIVING
WORLD

THE PHYSICAL
WORLD

EARTH and SPACE

TOOLS of SCIENCE

Observe

To watch, listen, smell, taste, or feel something to find out more about it.

Ella **observes** baby chickens at the zoo. They look yellow, they feel soft, and they make little "chirp" sounds.

Predict

To use what you already know to guess what might happen.

Miguel plants a seed in some soil. He **predicts** that it will grow into a plant.

Result

The thing that happens because of something else.

Joe put a ball on a hill. The **result** of this is that the ball rolled down the hill.

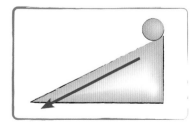

Safety

What you do to keep yourself from getting hurt.

You can wear **safety** goggles so your eyes don't get hurt.

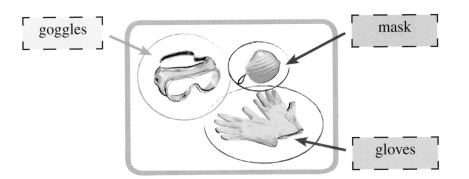

Technology

The use of science to make things that people need.

Scientists use **technology** to make new kinds of medicine.

Theory

An idea that most scientists agree with because it is backed up by evidence.

Scientists have a **theory** about the way planets move. They figured out that planets move in paths around a star.

9

Let's Get Scientific

Variable

Something in an experiment that can be changed.

The amount of light a plant gets can be a **variable**. It can be made different to see what happens to the plant.

Plant getting lots of light.

Plant getting little light.

Adapt

To change in a way that makes it easier to stay alive or be healthy.

Monkeys had to **adapt** to living in trees. They now have strong tails to help them climb.

The part of the animal that has changed is called an **adaptation**.

To help them climb in tall trees, monkeys have strong tails. These strong tails are an **adaptation**.

Animal

A living thing that has these traits:
Made of many cells
Can move around on its own
Needs oxygen to live
Eats other things that are alive or were alive

Some animals you may know are dogs, birds, fish, and frogs.

The Living World

Antibiotic

A medicine that kills bacteria. It will not work on a virus.

Kelly's cat was sick, so the doctor gave it an **antibiotic**.

Bacteria

A one-celled organism. They are not plants, but they are not animals, either. Some keep you healthy, but others can make you sick.

Bacteria are very small. You cannot see them with your eyes alone.

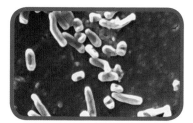

This is a picture of **bacteria** seen under a microscope.

Behavior

How a living thing acts.

Many birds build nests for their babies. Building nests is a **behavior** of birds.

Biosphere

All the parts of the Earth that have living things.

The **biosphere** starts very high up in the sky, where birds fly. It ends very deep in the ocean, where some fish live.

Biosphere

Camouflage

Something that allows a living thing to look like the area around it.

A polar bear has white fur so that it can hide in snow. This white fur is **camouflage** that helps the polar bear hide.

Carbon

The element found in all living things.

You can find **carbon** in animals and plants. When an animal eats a plant, the **carbon** moves from the plant into the animal and becomes part of it. When the animal dies, the **carbon** goes back into the ground. Then it might be used by a plant again. All living things use **carbon**.

Carbon dioxide

Waste that animals give off when they breathe out air. Plants use **carbon dioxide** to help them make food.

When you take a deep breath and blow out air, you are blowing out **carbon dioxide**.

Cell

What all living things are made of.

The living things that you can see are made of many **cells**, but some very small things are only made of one **cell**.

Many Cells

One Cell

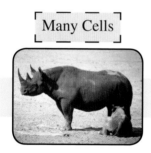

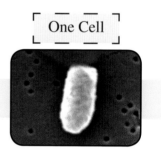

Chlorophyll

The green stuff inside green plants. It turns sunlight, water, and carbon dioxide into food for the plant.

Chlorophyll is what makes the leaves of plants green.

The Living World

Classify

To group things by ways they are the same.

You can **classify** living things into groups such as birds, fish, and flowers.

Flowers

Community

A group of plants and animals that live together in one place.

Frogs, fish, and many kinds of plants can live together in a pond **community**.

Fish

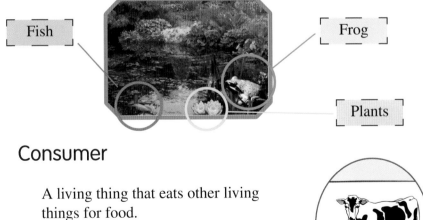

Frog

Plants

Consumer

A living thing that eats other living things for food.

A bird is a **consumer**. So is a cow.

Decomposer

A living thing that eats dead animals, dead plants, or waste.

Many bacteria are **decomposers**. A vulture is also a **decomposer**. A vulture eats things that have been dead for a while.

Ecosystem

A group of plants and animals that live together, along with the environment they live in.

Frogs, fish, plants, water, and rocks are all parts of a pond **ecosystem**.

Plants

Animals

Water

Endangered

In danger of no longer being alive.

The red wolf is **endangered**. There are fewer than 300 left in the world.

LET'S GET SCIENTIFIC

THE LIVING WORLD

THE PHYSICAL WORLD

EARTH and SPACE

TOOLS of SCIENCE

Environment

Everything that surrounds an animal or plant.

A deer's **environment** is the forest.

Extinct

When every one of a kind of living thing has died and there can be no more of them.

Dinosaurs are **extinct**. They are no longer living.

Food chain

The path that food moves through in an environment.

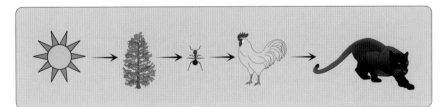

LET'S GET SCIENTIFIC

THE LIVING WORLD

THE PHYSICAL WORLD

EARTH and SPACE

TOOLS of SCIENCE

Fungi

The kingdom that includes mushrooms and molds.

Trish found some mushrooms on a log. They are all **fungi**.

The singular of **fungi** is **fungus**.

She sees one **fungus**.
I see three **fungi**.

Fungus

Fungi

Habitat

The place where a living thing lives.

This frog's **habitat** is a tree.

Interact

To act together and have an effect on each other.

Tess and her teacher **interact**. Tess listens to her teacher as the teacher speaks. When the teacher asks a question, Tess gives her the answer.

Kingdom

The biggest of the groups of living things.

Animals are one **kingdom**. Plants are another.

Some kingdoms include:

Animals,

Plants,

Fungi,

and Protists

Learned behavior

Something you have to learn to do.

You cannot ride a bicycle just by climbing onto one. You have to learn how to ride a bicycle. Bicycle riding is a **learned behavior**.

Many animals have **learned behaviors**, too. Some birds can learn how to open milk bottles. They do not know how to do this when they are born. They have to learn by watching other animals.

Life cycle

All of the ways a living thing changes as it grows from a baby to an adult that has babies of its own.

A frog's **life cycle** has many parts. First it is an egg. Then it becomes a tadpole. Next, it changes from a tadpole into an adult frog. Only adult frogs can make more frog eggs.

Living

Showing signs of being alive, such as growing.

Living system

Living things and their environment.

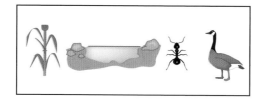

In a pond, plants get food from the soil, the water, and the sun. Some frogs and bugs eat the plants. The frogs and bugs also live in the water or on rocks near the water. All of the living and nonliving things work together. This is a **living system**.

Metamorphosis

A complete change into something else.

Caterpillars go through **metamorphosis** when they turn into butterflies.

Microorganism

A tiny living thing. Most are made of one cell.

Another word for **microorganism** is *microbe*.

You cannot see **microorganisms**, but they are all around us and they help us to live. Some **microorganisms** turn dead animals and plants into soil. Other **microorganisms** help people make bread. A few kinds of **microorganisms** can make you sick, but most kinds do not.

Natural world

Any part of the world not made by people.

The forest is part of the **natural world**. A building is not part of the **natural world**.

The **natural world** is sometimes just called *nature*.

Nonliving

Anything that does not show signs of life.

Rocks are **nonliving**. They do not grow, use food, or have offspring. Other things that are **nonliving** are cars, buildings, and water.

Nucleus

The part of a cell that tells it what to do.

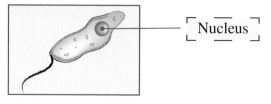

Nutrient

A part of food that helps a living thing grow.

The process of getting all of the **nutrients** you need is called *nutrition*.

The United States Department of Agriculture made a picture that can help you learn to eat well and have good nutrition.

Offspring

The children of living things.

The **offspring** of a pig is a piglet. Piglets grow up to be pigs just like their parents. Everything that is alive makes **offspring**.

Offspring

Organism

A living thing.

Each item shown below is an **organism**.

Oxygen

An element in the air that most living things need to stay alive.

You breathe **oxygen** into your lungs.

Parent

Any living thing that has offspring.

A pig is the **parent** of a piglet. You have **parents**, too.

Parent

Photosynthesis

The way that plants use energy from the Sun to make food.

Plants use **photosynthesis** to make food out of sunlight.

If you remember that "photo" means "light," it will help you remember that **photosynthesis** is how plants use light to make food.

Plant

The kingdom of living things that includes trees, flowers, and grass.

A tree is a **plant**. Flowers are also **plants**.

Predator

A living thing that hunts animals for food.

Owls are **predators**. They hunt small animals, such as mice, for food.

┌ ─ ─ ─ ┐
└ Predator ┘

Prey

An animal that becomes food for a predator.

A mouse can become **prey** for many animals such as owls or snakes.

┌ ─ ─ ─ ┐
└ Prey ┘

Producer

A living thing that makes its own food.

Plants are **producers**.

Protist

The kingdom of living things that includes algae and other one-celled organisms.

You cannot see most **protists**. Algae are **protists** that live in water in large groups. Even though you cannot see one of these **protists**, you can see many of them in a large group.

Reproduce

To make offspring.

Cats **reproduce** by making kittens. Some plants **reproduce** by making seeds that grow into new plants.

Species

A category of living things.

Living things are the same **species** when their offspring can make their own offspring.

Species is both a plural and singular word.

One Species

Many Species

Survive

To stay alive.

All living things need food and water to **survive**. Some animals need a place to live to **survive**.

Trait

Something in your body passed to you from your parents.

Brown eyes are a **trait** you might get if one of your parents has brown eyes.

Virus

A very small thing that makes a cell sick.

Viruses are not alive.

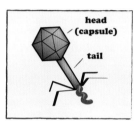

Real **viruses** are 100,000 times smaller than this picture.

Waste

What is left over when living things use something.

The parts of food that we don't eat are **waste**. Feces that comes from animals is also **waste**.

Boil

To change from a liquid to a gas.

Dad **boils** water to make tea. When the water **boils**, it starts to go into the air as vapor.

Buoyant

Able to float.

If you put a piece of cork in the water, it will float. Cork is **buoyant**. Boats are **buoyant**, too.

Circuit

A path that begins and ends in the same place, like a circle.

Electricity goes in a **circuit** made of wires.

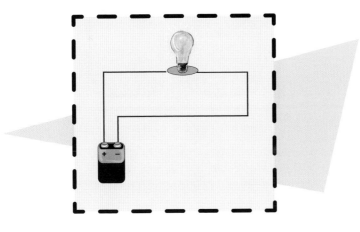

Complex

Complicated, hard, difficult.

Dad and I put a model airplane together. It took all day because it was **complex**.

Conduct

To move something along easily.

Metal **conducts** electricity. Metal allows electricity to move through it easily.

Density

How heavy something is compared to how much space it takes up.

A rock has a greater **density** than a foam ball.

Each of these items has a different **density**. The ball on the left is not very dense, so it floats. The rock on the right is more dense, so it sinks.

Dissolve

To mix something into a liquid. The thing you mix in seems to disappear into the liquid, but it is still there.

Sugar **dissolves** in water. You can't see the sugar after you mix it in water, but you can still taste it.

Electricity

A form of energy.

Electricity is the energy that makes a lamp turn on.

Element

The simplest thing that all other things are made from.

Carbon is an **element** that is found in all living things.

All of these things are made of **elements** like carbon.

Force

A push or pull.

Ken had to bring a box up a hill. He used **force** to push the box up the hill.

Freeze

To turn a liquid into a solid.

Water turns to ice when it is very cold. The water **freezes** and becomes ice.

Gas

A state of matter with no shape or volume.

When you open a bottle of perfume, the room will start to smell like the perfume. The perfume is a **gas** in the air that you can smell.

Gravity

The force that pulls two objects toward each other.

When you jump in the air, **gravity** is what pulls you back down.

Heat

A form of energy.

Things that have a lot of **heat** energy feel hot.

Lens

A piece of glass or plastic that focuses or spreads out light.

Microscopes and telescopes use **lenses** to help you see things that are very small or very far away.

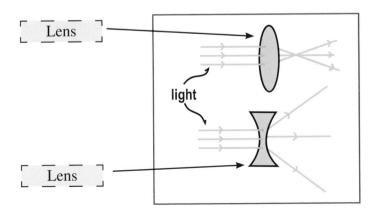

Lens

light

Lens

Light

Energy that lets us see.

A flashlight helps you see because it gives off **light**.

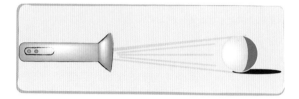

Liquid

A state of matter with a definite size, but no shape.

Water and oil are both **liquids**. You can measure how much water is in a cup, but the water is not the shape of the cup. If you take the water out of the cup, it goes everywhere. Water has a size that you can measure, but it has no shape.

Magnet

An object that can pull iron toward it.

A **magnet** on the refrigerator will hold up a note or a picture.

Magnetic

Acting like a magnet, or pulling toward iron, like a magnet does.

Some rocks are **magnetic**. They can pull iron toward them just like a magnet does. The Earth's poles are **magnetic**.

Mass

The amount of matter in something.

The more **mass** an object has, the harder it is for you to move it.

More mass   **Less mass**

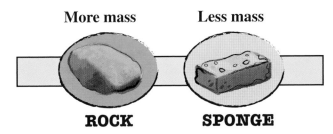

ROCK   **SPONGE**

Matter

Anything that has mass and takes up space.

You are made of **matter**. Everything you can see and touch is also made of **matter**.

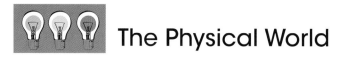

Melt

To turn from a solid into a liquid.

An ice cube **melts** in the sun.

Metal

Something that is shiny, bends without cracking, and can conduct heat and electricity.

Gold and silver are both **metals**. Coins are made of **metal**.

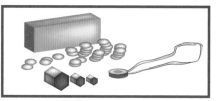

Mixture

A blend of two or more things. The two different items in the **mixture** do not change when blended.

If you mix sand and water, you can still see the sand in the water. The sand does not seem to disappear in a **mixture**.

Pattern

Something you see over and over again.

Bees build their honeycomb in a **pattern** of repeating shapes.

Physical property

Something you can know about an object using sight, taste, touch, smell, or hearing. The object does not change when you look at its **physical properties**.

Pole (magnetic)

Either end of a magnet, where the pull or push is strongest.

If you hold two magnets very close to each other, the **poles** will either push apart or they will pull together.

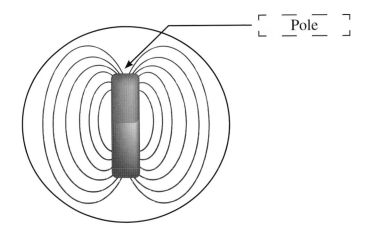

Pole

Power

How fast work can be done.

If two different trucks move bricks, the truck with more **power** will be able to move more bricks in the same amount of time.

Property

A characteristic of something.

Wood is hard. Hardness is a **property** of wood. Wood can burn. Being able to burn is another **property** of wood.

Reflect

To bounce off of a surface.

The mirror **reflects** light back to us.

Rotate

To turn about an axis.

A spinning top **rotates**. The Earth **rotates**, too.

Solid

A state of matter with definite size and shape.

Rocks, apples, and trees are all **solids**.

Solution

A liquid that has something dissolved in it.

When you pour sugar into water and stir it up, you have made a sugar and water **solution**.

Speed

How far something goes in a specific amount of time.

A fast car can go at a high **speed**.

States of matter

Nearly everything in the world is either a solid, a liquid, or a gas. These three together are called **states of matter**.

Which **state of matter** is water? Water is a liquid. Liquid is one **state of matter**. There are other **states of matter**, too. Solid and gas are other **states of matter**.

Symmetry

When something is exactly the same on one side as it is on the other, it has **symmetry**.

Each of these pictures has **symmetry**.

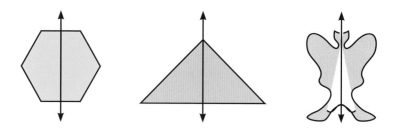

Texture

How something feels.

The **texture** of a tree is bumpy. The **texture** of glass is smooth.

Velocity

The speed and direction of a moving object.

The car goes 10 miles an hour moving north.

This is the car's **velocity**. Velocity is how fast something is going *and* the direction it is going.

Weight

How heavy something is, or the force of gravity.

The **weight** of a bowling ball is 10 pounds. This means that the Earth and the bowling ball are pulling on each other with 10 pounds of force.

LET'S GET SCIENTIFIC

THE LIVING WORLD

THE PHYSICAL WORLD

EARTH and SPACE

TOOLS of SCIENCE

Asteroid

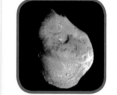

A very large rock in space.

There are lots of **asteroids** that go around our Sun. They are smaller than planets, but they are still very big.

Atmosphere

The layer of gas around a planet or a moon.

The Earth has an **atmosphere**. The air we breathe is part of Earth's **atmosphere**.

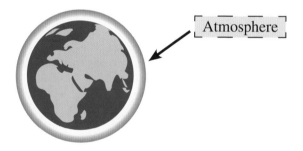

Atmosphere

Axis

An imaginary line that goes through the center of the Earth.

Earth spins on its **axis**.

Biosphere

All the parts of Earth with life.

The **biosphere** starts very high up in the sky, where birds fly. It ends very deep in the ocean, where some fish live.

Biosphere

LET'S GET SCIENTIFIC

THE LIVING WORLD

THE PHYSICAL WORLD

EARTH and SPACE

TOOLS of SCIENCE

Climate

The weather an area has most of the time.

Parts of North America have a hot and dry **climate**. The temperature is hot and the air is dry most of the time.

Comet

A big ball of ice and rock that orbits the Sun.

The ice in a **comet** turns to gas when it is heated by the sun. That is what makes a **comet's** tail.

Condensation

Water vapor coming out of the air and forming droplets.

If you put a cold glass of water on a table and watch it, you will see little drops of water form on the side. This water is coming out of the air and collecting on the glass. This is **condensation**.

Conserve

To use something wisely; also to not waste something natural.

You can **conserve** water by turning off the faucet when you brush your teeth. You can **conserve** paper by using both sides when you write.

Core

The center of the Earth.

The **core** is made of iron.

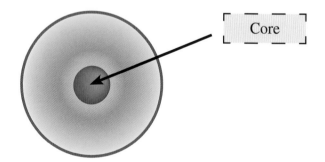

Crust

The outer rocky layer of the Earth.

The land we live on is part of the **crust** of the Earth. In an ocean, the **crust** is the land under the water.

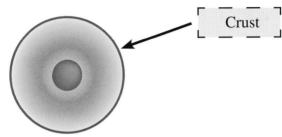

Crust

Current

The flow of a liquid, gas, or solid.

In a river, water flows in a **current**. It moves in one direction. Electricity flows in a **current** along wires.

Deposit

To leave something behind.

Ocean waves **deposit** shells and pebbles on the beach.

Earth

The third planet from the Sun.

Earth is the name of the planet we live on.

Earthquake

When the surface of the Earth moves suddenly.

In an **earthquake**, the ground starts to shake. This is because part of the crust of the Earth is moving.

Eclipse

A shadow that is caused by the Moon moving between the Earth and the Sun, or the Earth moving between the Sun and the Moon.

A lunar **eclipse** happens when the Earth's shadow is on the Moon. You can see the shadow move across the Moon.

A solar **eclipse** happens when the Sun is blocked in the daytime by the Moon. You should not look at a solar **eclipse** because the light can hurt your eyes.

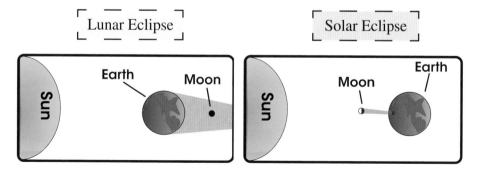

Environment

Everything that is around an animal or plant. Rocks, air, water, and living things are all part of the environment.

A deer's **environment** is the forest it lives in, the grass it walks on, the other animals it sees, and the water it drinks.

Erosion

When rock is slowly worn away by wind, water, or gravity.

Because of **erosion**, some mountains are not as tall as they used to be.

Evaporate

To change from liquid into vapor.

A puddle on the street will slowly go away. This is because the water **evaporates** into the air.

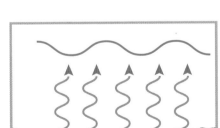

LET'S GET SCIENTIFIC

THE LIVING WORLD

THE PHYSICAL WORLD

EARTH and SPACE

TOOLS of SCIENCE

Fossil

A sign of a plant or animal that lived long ago.

Fossils include bones, leaves, and footprints.

Glacier

A huge river of ice that flows very slowly over the land.

Greenhouse effect

What happens when heat from the Sun cannot leave the Earth's atmosphere.

A greenhouse is a building made of glass that lets light and heat in and stays warm. These are used for growing plants. The term **greenhouse effect** comes from the way that the Earth's atmosphere acts like a greenhouse.

Lava

Very hot liquid rock that flows out of the surface of a planet.

The bright orange stuff flowing out of the ground in this picture is **lava**. **Lava** is made of rocks that are so hot, they have melted. **Lava** is orange because it is so hot, it glows.

Magma

Very hot liquid rock that is under a planet's surface.

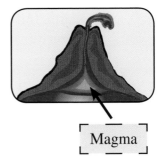

You can only find **magma** under the Earth's surface. If **magma** comes up to the surface through a hole in the ground, it becomes lava.

Magma

Mantle

A layer between a planet's crust and its core.

The Earth's **mantle** is made of solid rock.

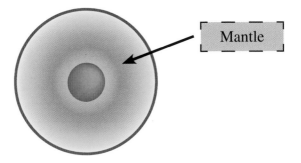

Mantle

Meteor

A rock from space that burns up as it falls through the atmosphere. They are sometimes called *shooting stars*.

This is a picture of a **meteor** shower. Lots of **meteors** are falling to Earth at one time.

Meteorite

A rock from space that lands on Earth's surface.

Usually, a meteor will burn up before it gets all the way to the Earth. If it doesn't burn up, the rock that is left is called a **meteorite**.

Moon

The natural satellite of a planet. **Moons** orbit their planets.

Earth has one **moon**, called the Moon. Other planets may have more than one **moon**. Jupiter has more than 50 **moons**. The four largest are named Io, Europa, Ganymede, and Callisto.

Earth's Moon

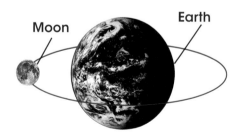

Moon

Earth

Nonrenewable resource

Anything that people use that they cannot put back, grow, or make quickly again.

Oil is a **nonrenewable resource**. Once we have burned all the oil on the Earth, we cannot make any more. There will be none left.

Orbit (noun)

In space, the path of one object around another object.

Earth's **orbit** goes around the Sun.

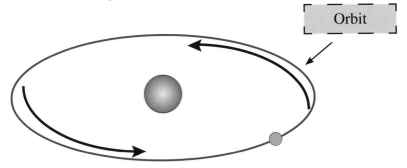

Orbit

Orbit (verb)

To go on a circular path around something in space.

The Earth **orbits** the Sun. The Moon **orbits** the Earth.

LET'S
GET
SCIENTIFIC

THE LIVING
WORLD

THE PHYSICAL
WORLD

EARTH and SPACE

TOOLS of SCIENCE

Planet

A large ball of rock or gas that moves around a star.

We live on a **planet**. Our **planet** is Earth.

Pole (geographic)

The point on the Earth's surface where its axis passes.

The Earth has two **poles**, the North Pole and the South Pole. Earth's **poles** are also magnetic, which means that a special magnet called a compass will point to one of the poles.

Pollute

To harm the Earth with waste.

If you throw trash on the ground, you have **polluted** the Earth. Throw trash in a garbage can so you do not **pollute** the Earth.

Pollution

Waste that is not natural and harms the Earth.

Anything that is not found in nature that is thrown on the ground is **pollution**. The smoke from cars and buildings that goes in the air is called air **pollution**.

Recycle

To use something again.

Many things, like soda cans, can be **recycled**. Soda cans are **recycled** by being melted and made into new things. You can **recycle** things like plastic bags by saving them and using them again.

Renewable resource

Any part of the environment that we use and can replace.

Trees are a **renewable resource**. As long as we are careful, we can plant new trees to replace the ones we use.

Satellite

In space, an object that travels around another object.

The moon is a **satellite** of Earth. Earth also has **satellites** that were made by people and sent into space. This is a picture of a **satellite** made by people.

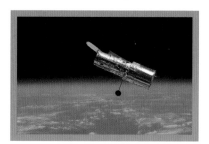

Soil

The layer of loose rocks and dead plants on Earth's surface. This is sometimes called dirt.

Plants grow in **soil**.

Solar system

A group of planets that moves around a star.

Our **solar system** has at least eight planets.

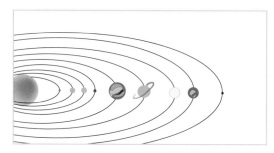

Space

All of the empty parts of the universe.

Star

A big ball of hot gases.

The closest **star** to Earth is the Sun.

Sun

The closest star to the Earth.

Earth orbits the **Sun**. The **Sun** gives us light and heat energy. We could not live without the **Sun**.

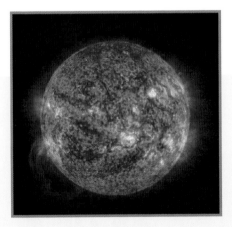

LET'S GET SCIENTIFIC

THE LIVING WORLD

THE PHYSICAL WORLD

EARTH and SPACE

TOOLS of SCIENCE

Volcano

A hole in the Earth where lava comes out. This word also means a mountain made of hardened lava.

In this picture, red-hot lava flows out of a **volcano**.

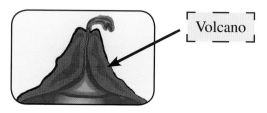

Volcano

Water cycle

The circle of water's flow from the land or ocean, into air, and back to land or ocean again.

This is a picture of the **water cycle**.

Weather

How warm, wet, and windy it is outside.

The **weather** today was bright and sunny. Tomorrow, the **weather** should be cold and rainy.

Weathering

How rocks and other things are worn away by weather.

When iron turns to rust, it gets brittle. Rain can make the brittle rust flake off and wash away. This is an example of **weathering**.

Balance

A tool for measuring mass or weight.

This tool gets its name from the fact that you **balance** different things on either side of it to figure out weight.

Calculator

A tool to help you do math.

 Eric wants to know how much a dozen eggs weigh. He weighs one egg. It is 60 grams. He uses his **calculator** to help him figure out 60 grams times 12 eggs. He figures out that a dozen eggs weigh about 720 grams.

Camera

A machine that takes pictures.

Alison brings her **camera** when she walks in the woods. She takes pictures of birds with her **camera**.

Chart

A picture that helps you understand information.

In our class, the teacher has a **chart** where we put the names of any animals we see on our class walks.

Amphibians	*Tree frog*	
Birds	*Woodpecker*	*Raven*
Mammals	*Deer*	*Fox*

Compass

A tool that shows you the direction you are facing.

A **compass** uses a magnet to tell you where North is. Once you know where North is, it is easier to figure out which way you are facing.

Computer

A machine that helps you find and sort information.

I looked for information about tigers on the **computer** at school. Then I used the **computer** to write a report about tigers.

Graph

A picture that shows how different things are related to each other.

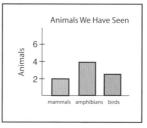

Hand lens

A pocket tool to help you see small things.

Jake uses a **hand lens** to look closely at an ant.

Map

A picture that helps you understand where things are.

This is a **map** of North America.

Meter stick

A tool used for measuring width, height, and distance in meters.

Our teacher used a **meter stick** to find out how wide our classroom is.

Microscope

A laboratory tool that helps you see very small things.

You can only see bacteria if you look at them with a **microscope**.

Ruler

A tool that helps you find out how long or tall something is. It also helps you draw straight lines.

Safety goggles

Glasses that protect your eyes.

When we mixed vinegar and water in class, our teacher made us wear **safety goggles**. That way, the vinegar wouldn't splash into our eyes.

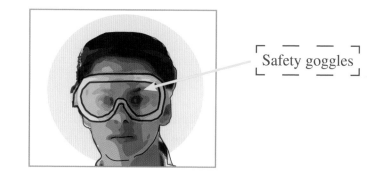

Safety goggles

Telescope

A tool that helps you see things that are very far away.

My dad and I look at stars at night with a **telescope**.

Test

A procedure for finding out more about something.

To figure out if a pile of white stuff is flour or sugar, you can do a **test**. Press on the pile. Sugar will feel crunchy. Flour will feel very soft.

Thermometer

A tool that measures temperature.

Timer

A machine that helps you figure out how long
something takes.

We used a **timer** to find out how long it takes for water
to boil.

LET'S
GET
SCIENTIFIC

THE LIVING
WORLD

THE PHYSICAL
WORLD

EARTH and SPACE

TOOLS of SCIENCE

Index

A

Adapt 11
Analyze 1
Animal 11
Antibiotic 12
Asteroid 42
Atmosphere 42
Axis 42

B

Bacteria 12
Balance 58
Behavior 12
Biosphere 13, 43
Boil 29
Buoyant 29

C

Calculator 58
Camera 58
Camouflage 13
Carbon 13
Carbon dioxide 14
Cell 14
Chart 59
Chlorophyll 14
Circuit 29
Classify 15
Climate 43
Comet 43
Community 15
Compass 59
Complex 30
Computer 59

Conclusion 1
Condensation 44
Conduct 30
Conserve 44
Constant 1
Consumer 15
Core 44
Crust 45
Current 45
Cycle 2

D

Data 2
Decomposer 16
Density 30
Deposit 45
Dissolve 31

E

Earth 46
Earthquake 46
Eclipse 46
Ecosystem 16
Electricity 31
Element 31
Endangered 16
Energy 2
Environment 17, 47
Erosion 47
Evaluate 3
Evaporate 47
Evidence 3
Examine 3

Index

Index

Credits

Many thanks to the following individuals and organizations for the use of their photography and/or illustrations in this publication:

CDC Global Health Odyssey, photographers Judy Gantt and Mary Hilpertshauser

Centers for Disease Control and Prevention PHIL, photographer Janice Carr

HubbleSite (NASA) http://hubblesite.org

Integration and Application Network, University of Maryland Center for Environmental Science, ian.umces.edu/symbols

http://gallery.spacebar.org, photographer Tom Murphy VII

Marine Mammal Commission

National Oceanic and Atmospheric Administration www.noaa.gov

National Park Service, Rocky Mountain National Park

North Dakota State University Department of Soil Science www.soilsci.ndsu.nodak.edu

OSHA www.osha.gov

Rutgers University http://rwqp.rutgers.edu/reg_priority/nutrient_man/

USDA Agricultural Research Service, photographer Jack Dykinga

US Fish and Wildlife Service

US Geologic Survey SOFIA (South Florida Information Access)

www.cepolina.com/freephoto

Additional Photo Credits
Photodisc, cover, i, (microscope); cover, i, (red tailed hawk)
Shutterstock, cover, i, Ewa Walicka, cover, i (plant in planter)

Notes

Notes

Notes

Notes

Notes

NO circ
7/11